POETRY FROM CRESCENT MOON

William Shakespeare: *Selected Sonnets and Verse*
edited, with an introduction by Mark Tuley

William Shakespeare: *The Sonnets*
edited and introduced by Mark Tuley

*Shakespeare: Love, Poetry and Magic
in Shakespeare's Sonnets and Plays*
by B.D. Barnacle

Edmund Spenser: *Heavenly Love: Selected Poems*
selected and introduced by Teresa Page

Robert Herrick: *Delight In Disorder: Selected Poems*
edited and introduced by M.K. Pace

Sir Thomas Wyatt: *Love For Love: Selected Poems*
selected and introduced by Louise Cooper

John Donne: *Air and Angels: Selected Poems*
selected and introduced by A.H. Ninham

D.H. Lawrence: *Being Alive: Selected Poems*
edited with an introduction by Margaret Elvy

D.H. Lawrence: Symbolic Landscapes
by Jane Foster

D.H. Lawrence: Infinite Sensual Violence
by M.K. Pace

Percy Bysshe Shelley: *Paradise of Golden Lights: Selected Poems*
selected and introduced by Charlotte Greene

Thomas Hardy: *Her Haunting Ground: Selected Poems*
edited, with an introduction by A.H. Ninham

Sexing Hardy: Thomas Hardy and Feminism
by Margaret Elvy

Emily Bronte: *Darkness and Glory: Selected Poems*
selected and introduced by Miriam Chalk

John Keats: *Bright Star: Selected Poems*
edited with an introduction by Miriam Chalk

Henry Vaughan: *A Great Ring of Pure and Endless Light: Selected Poems*
selected and introduced by A.H. Ninham

The Crescent Moon Book of Love Poetry
edited by Louise Cooper

The Crescent Moon Book of Mystical Poetry in English
edited by Carol Appleby

The Crescent Moon Book of Nature Poetry From Langland to Lawrence
edited by Margaret Elvy

The Crescent Moon Book of Metaphysical Poetry
edited and introduced by Charlotte Greene

The Crescent Moon Book of Elizabethan Love Poetry
edited and introduced by Carol Appleby

The Crescent Moon Book of Romantic Poetry
edited and introduced by L.M. Poole

Blinded By Her Light The Love-Poetry of Robert Graves
by Jeremy Mark Robinson

The Best of Peter Redgrove's Poetry: The Book of Wonders
by Peter Redgrove, edited and introduced by Jeremy Mark Robinson

Peter Redgrove: Here Comes the Flood
by Jeremy Mark Robinson

Sex-Magic-Poetry-Cornwall: A Flood of Poems
by Peter Redgrove, edited with an essay by Jeremy Mark Robinson

Brigitte's Blue Heart
by Jeremy Reed

Claudia Schiffer's Red Shoes
by Jeremy Reed

By-Blows: Uncollected Poems
by D.J. Enright

Petrarch, Dante and the Troubadours: The Religion of Love and Poetry
by Cassidy Hughes

Dante: *Selections From the Vita Nuova*
translated by Thomas Okey

Arthur Rimbaud: *Selected Poems*
edited and translated by Andrew Jary

Arthur Rimbaud: *A Season in Hell*
edited and translated by Andrew Jary

Rimbaud: Arthur Rimbaud and the Magic of Poetry
by Jeremy Mark Robinson

Friedrich Hölderlin: *Hölderlin's Songs of Light: Selected Poems*
translated by Michael Hamburger

Rainer Maria Rilke: *Dance the Orange:* Selected Poems
translated by Michael Hamburger

Rilke: Space, Essence and Angels in the Poetry of Rainer Maria Rilke
by B.D. Barnacle

German Romantic Poetry: Goethe, Novalis, Heine, Hölderlin, Schlegel, Schiller
by Carol Appleby

Arseny Tarkovsky: *Life, Life: Selected Poems*
translated by Virginia Rounding

Emily Dickinson: *Wild Nights: Selected Poems*
selected and introduced by Miriam Chalk

Cavafy: Anatomy of a Soul
by Matt Crispin

Delight In Disorder
Selected Poems

Delight In Disorder

Selected Poems

Robert Herrick

Edited by M.K. Pace

CRESCENT MOON

CRESCENT MOON PUBLISHING
P.O. Box 393
Maidstone
Kent, ME14 5XU
United Kingdom

First published 1996. Second edition 2008
Introduction © M.K. Pace, 1996, 2008.

Printed and bound in Great Britain.
Set in Garamond Book 12 on 18pt.
Designed by Radiance Graphics.

British Library Cataloguing in Publication data available

ISBN 1-86171-145-X
ISBN-13 9781861711458

Contents

The Argument of His Book

I sing of *Brooks*, of *Blossomes, Birds*, and *Bowers*:
Of *April, May*, of *June*, and *July-Flowers*.
I sing of *May-poles, Hock-carts, Wassails, Wakes*,
Of *Bride-grooms, Brides*, and of their *Bridall-cakes*.
I write of *Youth*, of *Love*, and have Accesse
By these, to sing of cleanly-*Wantonnesse*.
I sing of *Dewes*, of *Raines*, and piece by piece
Of *Balme*, of *Oyle*, of *Spice*, and *Amber-gris*.
I sing of *Times trans-shifting*; and I write
How *Roses* first came *Red*, and *Lillies White*.
I write of *Groves*, of *Twilights*, and I sing
The Court of *Mab*, and of the *Fairie-King*.
I write of *Hell*; I sing (and ever shall)
Of *Heaven*, and hope to have it after all.

To Meddowes

Ye have been fresh and green,
    Ye have been fill'd with flower:
And ye the Walks have been
    Where Maids have spent their houres.

You have beheld, how they
    With *Wicker Arks* did come
To kisse, and beare away
    The richer Couslips home.

Y'ave heard them sweetly sing,
    And seen them in a Round:
Each Virgin, like a Spring,
    With Hony-succles crown'd.

But now, we see, none here,
    Whose silv'rie feet did tread,
And with dishevell'd Haire,
    Adorn'd this smoother mead.

Like Unthrifts, having spent,
    Your stock, and needy grown,
Y'are left here to lament
    Your poore estates, alone.

To Blossoms

Faire pledges of a fruitful Tree,
    Why do ye fall so fast?
    Your date is not so past;
But you may stay yet here a while,
    To blush and gently smile;
        And go at last.

What, were ye borne to be
    An hour or half's delight;
    And so to bid goodnight?
'Twas pitie Nature brought ye forth
    Merely to show your worth,
        And lose you quite.

But you are lovely Leaves, where we
    May read how soon things have
    Their end, though ne'er so brave:
And after they have shown their pride,
    Like you a while: they Glide
        Into the Grave.

To Daffodils

Faire Daffodils, we weep to see
  You haste away so soon:
As yet the early-rising Sun
  Has not attain'd his Noon.
    Stay, stay,
    Until the hasting day
      Has run
    But to the Evensong:
And having pray'd together, we
    Will go with you along

We have short time to stay, as you,
  We have as short a Spring;
As quick a growth to meet Decay,
  As you, or anything.
    We die,
    As your hours do, and dry
      Away,
    Like to the Summer's rain;
Or as the pearls of Morning's dew,
    Ne'er to be found again.

The Succession of the Four Sweet Months

First, *April*, she with mellow showers
Opens the way for early flowers;
Then after her comes smiling *May*,
In a more rich and sweet array:
Next enters *June*, and brings us more
Jems, then those two, that went before:
Then (lastly) *July* comes, and she
More wealth brings in, then all those three.

Cherry Ripe

Cherry-ripe, ripe, ripe, I cry,
Full and fair ones; come, and buy:
If so be you ask me where
They do grow? I answer, there
Where my Julia's lips do smile; –
There's the land, or cherry-isle;
Whose plantations fully show
All the year where cherries grow.

The Wake

Come *Anthea* let us two
Go to Feast, as others do.
Tarts and Custards, Creams and Cakes,
Are the Junketts still at Wakes:
Unto which the Tribes resort,
Where the business is the sport:
Morris-dancers thou shalt see,
Marian too in Pagentrie:
And a Mimick to devise
Many grinning properties.
Players there will be, and those
Base in action as in clothes:
Yet with strutting they will please
The incurious Villages.
Near the dying of the day,
There will b a *Cudgell*-Play,
Where a *Coxomb* will be broke,
Ere a good *word* can be spoke:
But the anger ends all here,
Drench't in Ale, or drown'd in Beer.
Happy Rusticks, best content
With the cheapest Meriment:
And possess no other feare,
Then to want the Wake next Year.

The Lily in a Christal

You have beheld a smiling *Rose*
    When Virgins hands have drawn
    O'r it a Cobweb-Lawne:
And here, you see, this Lily shows,
    Tomb'd in a *Christal* stone,
More fair in this transparent case,
    Then when it grew alone;
    And had but single grace.

You see how *Cream* but naked is;
    Nor dances in the eye
    Without a Strawberrie:
Or some fine tincture, like to this,
    Which draws the sight thereto,
More by that wantoning with it;
    Then when the paler hue
    No mixture did admit.

You see how *Amber* through the streams
    More gently strokes the sight,
    With some conceal'd delight;
Then when he darts his radiant beams
    Into the boundless air:
Where either too much light his worth
    Doth all at once impair,
    Or set it little forth.

Put Purple Grapes, or Cherries in-
    To Glasse, and they will send
    More beauty to commend
Them, from that cleane and subtile skin,
    Then if they naked stood,
And had no other pride at all,
    But their own flesh and blood,
    And tinctures natural.

Thus Lily, Rose, Grape, Cherry, Cream,
    And Strawberrie do stir
    More love, when they transfer
A weak, a soft, a broken beam:
    Then if they sho'd discover
At full their proper excellence;
    Without some Scene cast over,
    To juggle with the sense.

Thus let this *Christal'd Lily* be
    A Rule, how far to teach,
    Your nakedness must reach:
And that, no further, then we see
    Those glaring colours laid
By Arts wise hand, but to this end
    They sho'd obey a shade;
    Lest they too far extend.

So though y'are white as Swan, or Snow,
And have the power to move
A world of men to love:
Yet, when your Lawns & Silks shall flow;
And that white cloud divide
Into a doubtful Twilight; then,
Then will your hidden Pride
Raise greater fires in men.

To Phillis *to Love, and Live With Him*

Live, live with me, and thou shalt see
The pleasures I'll prepare for thee:
What sweets the Country can afford
Shall blesse thy Bed, and blesse thy Board.
The soft sweet Mosse shall be thy bed,
With crawling Woodbine over-spread:
By which the silver-shedding streames
Shall gently melt thee into dreames.
Thy clothing next, shall be a Gowne
Made of the Fleeces purest Downe.
The tongues of Kids shall be thy meate;
Their Milke thy drinke; and thou shalt eate
The Pastes of Filberts for thy bread
With Cream of Cowslips buttered:
Thy Feasting-Tables shall be Hills
With *Daisies* spread, and *Daffadils*;
Where thou shalt sit, and *Red-brest* by,
For meat, shall give thee melody.
I'll give thee Chaines and Carkanets
Of *Primroses* and *Violets*.
A Bag and Bottle thou shalt have;
That richly wrought, and This as brave;
So that as either shall expresse
The Wearer's no meane Shepheardesse.
At Sheering-times, and yearely Wakes,
When *Themilis* his pastime makes,
There thou shalt be; and be the wit,

Nay more, the Feast, and grace of it.
On holy-dayes, when Virgins meet
To dance the Heyes with nimble feet;
Thou shalt come forth, and then appeare
Then *Queen of Roses* for that yeere.
And having danc't ('bove all the best)
Carry the Garland from the rest.
In Wicker-baskets Maids shall bring
To thee, (my dearest Shepharling)
The blushing Apple, bashfull Peare,
And shame-fac't Plum, (all simp'ring there).
Walk in the Groves, and thou shalt find
The name of *Phillis* in the Rind
Of every straight, and smooth-skin tree;
Where kissing that, I'll twice kisse thee.
To thee a Sheep-hook I will send,
Be-pranckt with Ribbands, to this end,
This, this alluring Hook might be
Lesse for to catch a sheep, then me.
Thou shalt have Possets, Wassails fine,
Not made of Ale, but spiced Wine;
To make thy Maids and selfe free mirth,
All sitting neer the glitt'ring hearth.
Thou sha't have Ribbands, Roses, Rings,
Gloves, Garters, Stockings, Shooes, and Strings
Of winning Colours, that shall move
Others to Lust, but me to Love.
These (nay) and more, thine own shall be,
If thou wilt love, and live with me.

The Vision to Electra

I dream'd we both were in a bed
Of Roses, almost smothered:
The warmth and sweetness had me there
Made lovingly familiar,
But that heard thy sweet breath say
Faults done by night will blush by day.
I kissed thee (panting), and I call
Night to the Record! that was all.
But, ah! if empty dreams so please,
Love give me more such nights as these.

Mrs Elizabeth Wheeler, *Under the Name*
of the Lost Sephardesse

Among the *Myrtles*, as I walkt,
Love and my sighs thus intertalkt:
Tell me, said I, in deep distresse,
Where I may find my Shepardesse.
Thou foole, said Love, know'st thou not this?
In every thing that's sweet, she is.
In yond' *Carnation* go and seek,
There thou shalt find her lip and cheek:
In that ennamel'd *Pansie* by,
There thou shalt have her curious eye:
In bloome of *Peach*, and *Roses* bud,
There waves the Streamer of her blood.
'Tis true, said I, and thereupon
I went to pluck them one by one,
To make of parts an union;
But on a sudden all were gone.
At which I stopt; Said Love, these be
The true resemblances of thee;
For as these flowers, thy joyes must die,
And in the turning of an eye;
And all thy hopes of her must wither,
Like those short sweets ere knit together.

from *The Apparition of His Mistress Calling Him to Elysium*

Come then, and like two Doves with silv'ry wings,
Let our souls fly to th' shades where ever springs
Sit smiling in the Meads; where Balm and Oil,
Roses and cassia crown the untill'd soil.
Where no disease reigns, or infection comes
To blast the Air, but *Ambergris* and *Gums*.
This, that, and ev'ry Thicket doth transpire
More sweet than *Storax* from the hallowed fire;
Where ev'ry tree a wealthy issue bears
Of fragrant Apples, blushing Plums, or Peares;
And all the shrubs, with sparkling spangles, show
Like Morning Sunshine tinselling the dew.
Here in green Meddowes sits eternal May,
Purfling the Margents, while perpetual Day
So double gilds the Air, as that no night
Can ever rust th'Enamel of the light.
Here, naked Younglings, handsome Striplings, run
Their Goales for Virgins' kisses; which when done,
Then unto Dancing forth the learned Round
Commix'd they meet, with endless Roses crown'd.
And here we'll sit on Primrose-banks, and see
Love's *Chorus* led by *Cupid*; and we'll be
Two loving followers, too, unto the Grove
Where Poets sing the stories of our love.

His Mistress To Him At His Farewell

You may vow I'll not forget
To pay the debt
Which to thy memory stands as due
As faith can seal it you.
  – Take then tribute of my tears;
So long as I have fears
To prompt me, I shall ever
Languish and look, but thy return see never.
Oh then to lessen my despair,
Print thy lips into(the air,
So by this
Means, I may kiss thy kiss,
Whenas some kind
Wind
Shall hither waft it: – And, in lieu,
My lips shall send a thousand back to you.

To the most fair and lovely Mistress,
Anne Soame, *now* Lady Abdie

So smell those odours that do rise
From out the wealthy spiceries:
So smells the flower of *blooming Clove*;
Or *Roses* smother'd in the stove:
So smells the Aire of spiced wine;
Or *Essences* of *Jessimine*:
So smells the Breath about the hives,
When well the work of honey thrives;
And all the *busie Factours* come
Laden with wax and honey home:
So smell those neat and woven Bowers,
All over-archt with *Orange flowers*,
And *Almond blossoms*, that do mix
To make rich these *Aromatikes*:
So smell those bracelets, and those bands
Of *Amber* chaf't between the hands,
When thus enkindled they transpire
A noble perfume from the fire.
The wine of cherries, and to these,
The cooling breath of Respasses;
The smell of mornings milk, and cream;
Butter of *Cowslips* mixt with them;
Of roasted warden, or bak'd pear,
These are not to be reckon'd here;
When as the meanest part of her,
Smells like the maiden-Pomander.

Thus sweet she smells, or what can be
More lik'd by her, or lov'd by me.

Love Lightly Pleased

Let fair or foul my mistress be,
Or low, or tall, she pleaseth me;
Or let her walk, or stand, or sit,
The posture her's, I'm pleased with it;
Or let her tongue be still, or stir
Graceful is every thing from her;
Or let her grant, or else deny,
My love will fit each history.

Of Love: A Sonnet

How Love came in, I do not know,
Whether by th'eye, or ear, or no;
Or whether with the soul it came,
At first, infused with the same;
Whether in part 'tis here or there,
Or, like the soul, whole every where.
This troubles me; but I as well
As any other, this can tell;
That when from hence she does depart,
The outlet then is from the heart.

His Protestation to Perilla

Noonday and Midnight shall at once be seen:
Trees, at one time, shall be both sere and green:
Fire and water shall together lie
In one self-sweet-conspiring sympathy:
Summer and Winter shall at one time show
Ripe ears of corn, and up to th' ears in snow:
Seas shall be sandless; fields devoid of grass;
Shapeless the world, (as when all *Chaos* was)
Before my dear *Perilla*, I will be
False to my vow, or fall away from thee.

To Anthea

Come *Anthea*, know thou this,
Love at no time idle is:
Let's be doing, though we play
But at push-pin (half the day:)
Chains of sweetbents let us make,
Captive one, or both, to take:
In which bondage we will lie,
Soules transfusing thus, and die.

Art Above Nature; To Julia

When I behold a Forest spread
With silken trees upon thy head,
And when I see that other Dress
Of flowers set in comeliness:
When I behold another grace
In the ascent of curious Lace,
Which like a Pinnacle doth show
The top, and the top-gallant too.
Then, when I see thy Tresses bound
Into an Oval, square, or round;
And knit in knots far more than I
Can tell by tongue, or true-love tie:
Next, when those Lawny Films I see
Play with a wild civility:
And all those airy silks to flow,
Alluring me, and tempting so:
I must confess, mine eye and heart
Dotes less on Nature, than on Art.

To Julia

Permit me, *Julia*, now to go away;
Or by thy love, decree me here to stay.
If thou wilt say, that I shall live with thee;
Here shall my endless Tabernacle be:
If not, (as beautiful) I will live alone
There, where no language ever yet was known.

To Julia

How rich and pleasing thou my *Julia* art
In each thy dainty, and peculiar part!
First, thy *Queen-ship* on thy head is set
Of flowers a sweet commingled Coronet:
About thy neck a Carkanet is bound,
Made of the *Rubie, Pearle* and *Diamond*:
A golden ring, that shines upon thy thumb:
About thy wrist, the rich *Dardanium*.
Between thy Breasts (than Down of Swans more
                                white)
There plays the *Sapphire* with the *Chrysolite*.
No part besides must of thy selfe be known,
But by the *Topaz, Opal, Calcedon*.

Upon Julia's *Unlacing Herself*

Tell, if thou canst, (and truly) whence doth come
This *Camphire, Storax, Spiknard, Galbanum*:
These *Musks*, these *Ambers*, and those other smells
(Sweet as the *vestrie of the Oracles*.)
I'll tell thee; while my *Julia* did unlace
Her silken bodies, but a breathing space:
The passive Aire such odour then assum'd,
As when to *Jove* Great *Juno* goes perfum'd.
Whose pure-Immortal body doth transmit
A scent, that fills both Heaven and Earth with it.

The Night-Piece to Julia

Her Eyes the Glow-worm lend thee,
The Shooting Starres attend thee;
          And the Elves also,
          Whose little eyes glow
Like the sparks of fire, befriend thee.

No *Will-o'-the-Wispe* mislight thee,
Nor Snake or Slow-worm bite thee;
          But on, on thy way
          Not making a stay,
Since Ghost there's none to affright thee.

Let not the dark thee cumber:
What though the Moon does slumber?
          The Starres of the night
          Will lend thee their light
Like Tapers clear without number.

Then *Julia*, let me woo thee,
Thus, thus to come unto me;
          And when I shall meet
          Thy silv'ry feet
My soul I'll pour into thee.

The Maiden-blush

So look the mornings when the Sun
Paints them with fresh Vermilion:
So Cherries blush, and Kathern Peares,
And Apricocks, in youthful yeares:
So Corralls looke more lovely Red,
And Rubies lately polished:
So purest Diaper doth shine,
Stain'd by the Beames of Claret wine:
As *Julia* looks when she doth dress
Her either cheeke with bashfulness.

Julia's *Petticoat*

Thy Azure Robe I did behold,
As airy as the leaves of gold,
Which, erring here, and wand'ring there,
Pleas'd with transgression everywhere:
Sometimes 'twould pant, and sigh, and heave,
As if to stir it scarce had leave:
But having got it; thereupon
'Twould make a brave expansion.
And pound'd with stars it show'd to me
Like a *Celestiall Canopie*.
Sometimes 'twould blaze, and then abate,
Like to a flame grown moderate:
Sometimes away 'twould wildly fling,
Then to thy thighs so closely cling
That some conceit did melt me down,
As lovers fall into a swoon:
And, all confus'd, I there did lie
Drown'd in Delights, but could not die.
That Leading Cloud I follow'd still,
Hoping t'have seen of it my fill;
But ah! I could not: should it move
To Life Eternal, I could love.

Upon Julia's *Clothes*

When as in silks my *Julia* goes,
Then, then (me thinks) how sweetly flowes
That liquefaction of her clothes.

Next, when I cast mine eyes and see
That brave Vibration each way free;
O how that glittering taketh me!

To Julia, *in Her Dawn, or Daybreak*

By the next kindling of the day
   My *Julia* thou shalt see,
Ere *Ave-Mary* thou canst say
   I'll come and visit thee.

Yet ere thou counsl'st with thy Glasse,
   Appeare thou to mine eyes
As smooth, and nak't, as she that was
   The prime of *Paradise*.

If blush thou must, then blush thou through
   A Lawn, that thou mayst looke
As purest Pearles, or Pebbles do
   When peeping through a Brooke.

As Lilies shrin'd in Christall, so
   Do thou to me appeare;
Or Damask Roses, when they grow
   To sweet acquaintance there.

Delight in Disorder

A sweet disorder in the dress
Kindles in clothes a wantonness:
A Lawn about the shoulders thrown
Into a fine distraction:
An erring Lace which here and there
Enthralls the Crimson Stomacher:
A Cuff neglectful, and thereby
Ribands to flow confusedly:
A winning wave (deserving Note)
In the tempestuous petticoat:
A careless shoestring, in whose tie
I see a wild civility:
Do more bewitch me, than when Art
Is too precise in every part.

A Meditation For His Mistress

You are a *Tulip* seen today,
But (Dearest) of so short a stay
That where you grew scarce man can say.

You are a lovely *July-flower*
Yet one rude wind or ruffling shower
Will force you hence, (and in an hour.)

You are a sparkling *Rose* in' th'bud,
Yet lost ere that chaste flesh and blood
Can show where you or grew or stood.

You are a full-spread, fair-set Vine,
And can with Tendrils love entwine,
Yet dry'd, ere you distil your Wine.

You are like Balme enclosed (well)
In *Amber*, or some *Crystal* shell,
Yet lost ere you transfuse your smell.

You are a dainty *Violet*,
Yet whither'd ere you can be set
Within a Virgin's Coronet.

You are the *Queen* all flowers among,
But die you must (fair Maid) ere long,
As He, the maker of this song.

To His Mistress (Objecting to Him Neither Toying or Talking)

You say I love not, 'cause I do not play
Still with your curls, and kiss the time away.
You blame me too, because I can't devise
Some sport, to please those Babies in your eyes:
By *Love's Religion*, I must here confess it,
The most I love, when I the least express it.
Small griefs find tongues: Full Casks are ever found
To give (if any, yet) but little sound.
Deep waters noiseless are; and this we know,
That chiding streams betray small depth below.
So when Love speechless is, she doth expresse
A depth in love, and that depth, bottomlesse.
Now since my love is tongueless, know me such,
Who speak but little, 'cause I love so much.

A *Conjuration, to* Electra

By those soft Tods of wool
With which the air is full:
By all those Tinctures there,
That paint the *Hemisphere*:
By Dews and drizzling Rain,
That swell the Golden Grain:
By all those sweets that he
I' the flow'ry Nunnery:
By silent Nights, and the
Three Forms of Hecate:
By all Aspects that bless
The sober *Sorceress*,
While juice she strains, and pith
To make her Philtres with:
By Time, that hastens on
Things to perfection:
And by your self, the best
Conjurement of the rest:
Of my *Electra*! be
In love with none, but me.

To Electra

I dare not ask a kisse;
   I dare not beg a smile;
Lest having that, or this,
   I might grow proud the while.

No, no, the utmost share
   Of my desire, shall be
Only to kisse that Aire,
   That lately kissed thee.

Lovers, How They Come and Part

A *Gyges'* Ring they bear about them still,
To be, and not seen when and where they will.
They tread on clouds, and though they sometimes fall,
They fall like dew, but make no noise at all.
So silently they one to th'other come,
As colours steal into the Pear or Plum,
And Air-like, leave no pression to be seen
Where e'er they met, or parting place has been.

To Sylvia, To Wed

Let us, though late, at last, my Silvia, wed;
And loving lie in one devoted bed.
Thy watch may stand, my minutes fly post haste;
No sound calls back the year that once is past.
Then, sweetest Silvia, let's no longer stay;
True love, we know, precipitates delay.
Away with doubts, all scruples hence remove!
No man, at one time, can be wise, and love.

On a Perfumed Lady

You say you're sweet: how should we know
Whether that you be sweet or no?
 – From powders and perfumes keep free;
Then we shall smell how sweet you be!

To the Maids to Walk Abroad

Come sit we under yonder Tree,
Where merry as the Maids we'll be.
And as on *Primroses* we sit,
We'll venter (if we can) at wit:
If not, at *Draw-gloves* we will play;
So spend some minutes of the day:
Or else spin out the thread of sands,
Playing at *Questions* and *Commands*:
Or tell what strange Tricks Love can do,
By quickly making one of two.
Thus we will sit and talk; but tell
No cruel truths of *Philomell*,
Of *Phillis*, whom hard Fate forc't on,
To kill her selfe for *Demophon*.
But Fables we'll relate; how *Jove*
Put on all shapes to get a Love:
As now a *Satyr*, then a *Swan*;
A *Bull* but then; and now a man.
Next we will act, how young men woe;
And sigh, and kiss, as Lovers do:
And talk of Brides; & who shall make
That wedding-smock, this bridal-Cake;
That Dress, this Sprig, that Leaf, this Vine;
That smooth and silken Columbine.
This done, we'll draw lots, who shall buy
And guild the Baies and Rosemary:

What Posies for our Wedding Rings;
What Gloves we'll give, and Ribanings:
And smiling at ourselves, decree,
Who then the joining *Priest* shall be.
What short sweet Prayers shall be said;
And how the Possets all be made
With Cream of Lilies (not of Kine)
And *Maiden's-blush*, for spiced wine.
Thus, having talkt, we'll next commend
A kiss to each; and *so we'll end*.

Corinna's *Going a-Maying*

Get up, get up for shame, the Blooming Morn
Upon her wings presents the god unshorn.
      See how *Aurora* throws her fair
      Fresh-quilted colours through the air:
      Get up, sweet-Slug-a-bed, and see
      The Dew bespangled Herb and Tree.
Each flower has wept and bow'd towards the East
Above an hour since: yet you not dress'd;
      Nay! not so much as out of bed?
      When all the birds have Matins said
      And sung their thankful Hymns, 'tis sin,
      Nay, profanation to keep in,
When as a thousand Virgins on this day
Spring, sooner than the Lark, to fetch in May.

Rise and put on your Foliage, and be seen
To come forth, like the Spring-time, fresh and green,
      And sweet as *Flora*. Take no care
      For jewels for your Gown or Hair:
      Fear not; the leaves will strew
      Gems in abundance upon you:
Besides, the childhood of the Day has kept,
Against you come, some *Orient Pearls* unwept;
      Come and receive them while the light
      Hangs on the Dew-locks of the night:
      And *Titan* on the Eastern hill

Retires himself, or else stands still
Till you come forth. Wash, dress, be brief in praying:
Few Beads are best when once we go a-Maying.

Come, my *Corinna*, come; and, coming, mark
How each field turns a street, each street a Park
        Made green and trimm'd with trees: see
                  how
        Devotion gives each House a Bough
        Or Branch: Each Porch, each door ere this
        An Ark, a Tabernacle is,
Made up of white-thorn neatly interwove;
As if here were those cooler shades of love.
        Can such delights be in the street
        And open fields and we not see't?
        Come, we'll abroad; and let's obey
        The Proclamation made for May:
And sin no more, as we have done, by staying;
But, my *Corinna*, come, let's go a-Maying.

There's not a budding Boy or Girl this day
But is got up, and gone to bring in May.
        A deal of youth, ere this, is come
        Back, and with *White-thorn* laden home.
        Some have despatch'd their Cakes and
                Cream
        Before that we have left to dream:
And some have wept, and woo'd, and plighted Troth,
And chose their Priest, ere we can cast off sloth:
        Many a green-gown has been given;

Many a kiss, both odd and even:
Many a glance too has been sent
From out the eye, Love's Firmament;
Many a jest told of the Keys betraying
This night, and Locks pick'd, yet we're not a-Maying.

Come, let us go while we are in our prime;
And take the harmless folly of the time,
We shall grow old apace, and die
Before we know our liberty.
Our life I short, and our days run
As fast away as does the sun;
And, as a vapour or a drop of rain,
Once lost, can ne'er be found again,
So when or you or I are made
A fable, song, or fleeting shade,
All love, all liking, all delight
Lies drowned with us in endless night.
Then while time serves, and we are but decaying,
Come, my *Corinna*, come, let's go a-Maying.

Another Grace For A Child

Here a little child I stand
Heaving up my either hand;
Cold as paddocks though they be,
Here I lift them up to Thee,
For a benison to fall
On our meat, and on us all. Amen.

To Music. A Song

Music, thou *Queen of Heaven*, Care-charming-spell,
    That strik'st a stilnesse into hell:
Thou that tam'st *Tygers*, and fierce storms (that rise)
    With thy soul-melting Lullabies:
Fall down, down, down, from those thy chiming
                           spheres,
To charme our soules, as thou enchant'st our eares.

To the Virgins, to Make Much of Time

Gather ye Rose-buds while ye may,
  Old Time is still a flying:
And this same flower that smiles today,
  Tomorrow will be dying.

The glorious Lamp of Heaven, the Sun,
  The high he's a getting;
The sooner will his Race be run,
  And nearer he's to Setting.

That Age is best, which is the first,
  When Youth and Blood are warmer;
But being spent, the worse, and worst
  Times, still succeed the former.

Then be not coy, but use your time;
  And while ye may, goe marry:
For having lost but once your prime,
  You may forever tarry.

The Eye

Make me a heaven; and make me there
Many a less and greater spheare.
Make me the straight, and oblique lines;
The Motions, Lations, and the Signes.
Make me a Chariot, and a Sun;
And let them through a Zodiac run:
Next, place me Zones, and Tropicks there;
With all the Seasons of the Yeare.
Make me a Sun-set; and a Night:
And then present the Mornings-light
Cloath'd in her Chamlets of Delight.
To these, make Clouds to poure downe raine;
With weather foule, then faire againe.
And when, wise Artist, that thou hast,
With all that can be, this heaven grac't;
Ah! what is then this curious skie,
But only my *Corinna's* eye?

His Return to London

From the dull confines of the drooping West,
To see the day spring from the pregnant East,
Ravisht in spirit, I come, nay more, I flie
To thee, blest place of my Nativitie!
Thus, thus with hallowed foot I touch the ground,
With thousand blessings by thy Fortune crown'd.
O fruitful Genius! that bestowest here
An everlasting plenty, yeere by yeere.
O *Place! O People!* Manners! fram'd to please
All *Nations, Customes, Kindreds, Languages!*
I am a free-born *Roman*; suffer then,
That I amongst you live a Citizen.
London my home is: though by hard fate sent
Into a long and irksome banishment;
Yet since call'd back; henceforward let me be,
O native country, repossest by thee!
For, rather then I'll to the West return,
I'll beg of thee first here to have mine Urn.
Weak I am grown, and must in short time fall;
Give thou my sacred Reliques Burial.

His Tears to Thamasis

I send, I send here my supremest kiss
To thee my *silver-footed Thamasis*.
No more shall I reiterate thy Strand,
Whereon so many Stately Structures stand:
Nor in the summers sweeter evenings go,
To bath in thee (as thousand others doe.)
No more shall I along thy christall glide,
In Barge (with boughs and rushes beautifi'd)
With soft-smooth Virgins (for our chast disport)
To *Richmond, Kingstone*, and to *Hampton-Court*:
Never again shall I with Finnie-Ore
Put from, or draw unto the faithful shore:
And Landing here, or safely Landing there,
Make way to my *Beloved Westminster*:
Or to the *Golden-cheap-side*, where the earth
Of *Julia Herrick* gave to me my Birth.
May all clean *Nymphs* and curious water Dames,
With Swan-like-state, float up & down thy streams:
No drought upon thy wanton waters fall
To make them Leane, and languishing at all.
No ruffling winds come hither to disease
Thy pure, and *Silver-wristed Naides*.
Keep up your state ye streams; and as ye spring,
Never make sick your Banks by surfeiting.
Grow young with Tides, and though I see ye never,
Receive this vow, *so fare-ye-well for ever*.

Poets

Wantons we are; and though our words be such,
Our Lives do differ from our Lines by much.

On Love

Love's of itself too sweet; the best of all
Is, when love's honey has a dash of gall.

Silence

Suffer thy legs, but not thy tongue to walk:
God, the most Wise, is sparing of His talk.

Presence and Absence

When what is lov'd, is Present, love doth spring;
But being absent, Love lies languishing.

Another Upon Her Weeping

She by the River sat, and sitting there,
She wept, and made it deeper by a teare.

Dreams

Here we are all, by day; By night, w'are hurl'd
By dreams, each one, into a sev'rall world.

Life Is the Body's Light

Life is the body's light; which, once declining,
Those crimson clouds i' th' cheeks and lips leave
                              shining:-
Those counter-changed tabbies in the air,
The sun once set, all of one colour are:
So, when death comes, fresh tinctures lose their
                              place,
And dismal darkness then doth smutch the face.

Discontents In Devon

More discontents I never had
Since I was born, than here;
Where I have been, and still am, sad,
In this dull Devonshire.
Yet justly too I must confess,
I ne'er invented such
Ennobled numbers for the press,
Than where I loath'd so much.

The Departure of the Good Dæmon

What can I do in Poetry,
Now the good Spirit's gone from me?
Why nothing now, but lonely sit,
And over-read what I have writ.

His Poetrie His Pillar

Only a little more
    I have to write,
    Then I'll give o're,
And bid the world Goodnight.

'Tis but a flying minute,
    That I must stay,
    Or linger in it;
And then I must away.

O time that cut'st down all!
    And scarce leav'st here
    Memorial
Of any men that were.

How many lye forgot
    In Vaults beneath?
    And piecemeal rot
Without a fame in death?

Behold this living stone,
    I fear for me,
    Ne'r to be thrown
Downe, envious Time by thee.

Pillars let some set up,
    (If so they please)
    Here is my hope,
And my *Pyramids*.

To Find God

Weigh me the fire; or canst thou find
A way to measure out the Wind;
Distinguish all those Floods that are
Mix'd in that watrie theatre;
And taste thou them as saltlesse there
As in their channel first they were.
Tell me the People that do keep
Within the Kingdoms of the Deep;
Or fetch me back that Cloud again
Beshiver'd into seeds of Rain;
Tell me the motes, dust, sands, and spears
Of corn, when Summer shakes his ears;
Show me that world of Starres, and whence
They noiseless spill their Influence:
This if thou canst, then show me Him
That rides the glorious *Cherubim*.

On Heaven

Permit mine eyes to see
Part, or the whole of Thee,
   O happy place!
   Where all have Grace,
   And Garlands shar'd,
   For their reward;
   Where each chaste Soul
   In long, white stole,
   And Palmes in hand,
   Do ravisht stand;
   So in a ring,
   The praises sing
   Of Three in One,
   That fill the Throne;
While Harps, and Viols then
To Voices, say, *Amen.*

Eternitie

O years! and Age! Farewell:
    Behold I go,
    Where I do know
Infinitie to dwell.

And these mine eyes shall see
    All times, how they
    Are lost i'th'Sea
Of vast Eternitie.

Where never Moone shall sway
    The Starres; but she,
    And Night, shall be
Drown'd in one endlesse Day.

Upon Parting

Go hence away, and in thy parting know
Tis not my voice, but heavens, that bids thee go;
Spring hence thy faith, nor thinke it ill desert
I find in thee, that makes me thus to part,
But voice of fame, and voice of heaven have
thunder'd
We both were, if both of us not sunder'd;
Fold now thine arms, and in thy last look reare
One Sigh of love, and coole it with a teare;
Since part we must Let's kisse, that done retire
With as cold frost, as erst we met with fire;
With such white vows as fate can ne'er dissever
But truth knit fast; and so farewell for ever.

To His Booke

Go thou forth my booke, though late;
Yet be timely fortunate.
It may chance good-luck may send
Thee a kinsman, or a friend,
That may harbour thee, when I,
With my fates neglected lye.
If thou know'st not where to dwell,
See, the fire's by: *Farewell*.

A Note On Robert Herrick

ROBERT HERRICK (1591-1674) was one of the Cavalier poets (other Cavalier poets included Suckling, Carew and Lovelace). He was born in London and lived much of his life in the rough remoteness of a parish in Devonshire. He studied at Cambridge (St John's College and Trinity Hall), graduating in 1617 as a Bachelor of Arts and a Master of Arts in 1620. His law studies were dropped in 1623, and he was ordained as a deacon and priest in 1624. His major work (*Hesperides or The Works both Humane and Divine* of Robert Herrick Esq.) was published in 1648. There are some 1130 poems in the first, secular part, *Hesperides*, and 272 in *Noble Numbers*, the religious works. F.R. Leavis reckoned that Herrick was 'trivially charm-ing',[1] a view easily refuted by any close perusal of his verse. For T.S. Eliot, Herrick was the paradigmatic 'minor poet'.[2] One can understand how it is that Herrick was for so long viewed in this way. The more one considers his *Hesperides*, though, which one recent critic called 'a seductively sweet, strangely tumultuous exploration of love, art, friendship, festivity, and loss',[3] the greater Robert Herrick becomes.

One of the delights included in this book is Robert Herrick's magnificent 'The Argument of His Book'. This is a truly majestic fourteen-line poem, an invocation to Nature, and of humans interacting with Nature. It is, essentially, a list-poem, where the poet catalogues the things he will sing about in the rest of his book:

I sing of *Brooks*, of *Blossomes, Birds,* and *Bowers*:
Of *April, May,* of *June,* and *July*-Flowers.
I sing of *May-poles, Hock-carts, Wassails, Wakes,*
Of *Bride-grooms, Brides,* and of their *Bridall-cakes.*
I write of *Youth*, of *Love*, and have Accesse
By these, to sing of cleanly-*Wantonesse.*

Herrick couches his list in simple, dramatic English, a form of direct, powerful English that people since Herrick's time have associated with the (King James) Bible. The rest of his poetry (in his *Hesperides*) followed the plan outlined the poem 'The Argument of His Book'. Herrick was particularly well situated, geographically, to write Nature poetry. Like Coleridge, Wordsworth and Brontë, Herrick lived in the midst of the countryside – in the relative isolation of Dean Prior, on the edge of Dartmoor in Devon (he compared his exile with that of Ovid and Horace). Herrick lived in the vicarage in the village halfway between Exeter and Plymouth from 1630 to 1648, and from 1660 to his death, at 83, in 1674. Though at times he fought against the isolation and roughness of his provincial setting,[4] and hankered after the civilization of London, one can see the deep inspiration that the landscape of Devonshire had for Herrick in his poetry. Exiled from the capital and civilized society and culture, Herrick did have his books (his beloved Bible and Latin poets) as well as the friendship of his pets (they appear in his poems, sometimes in heartfelt elegies when they die – such as 'Upon His Spaniel Tracie'), his housekeeper (Prudence Baldwin), his sister, and friends at the nearby Dean Court.

For mediæval, Renaissance and Cavalier poets (like Herrick) Britain would have been a much more 'pastoral' landscape than it is in the 20th century. There would have many more trees, far fewer roads, no cars, planes, trains, electric lights, pylons, pipes, road signs, telephones, and so on. The landscape that poets such as Langland, Chaucer, Wyatt, Parnell, Smith, Keats and Brontë lived in was dramatically different from the urbanized world of the 20th century. There are, of course, continuities between the mediæval and Elizabethan period and now: the same rivers flow, the same birds sing (minus a few species), the same trees rustle their leaves in Autumn. It is (partly) this continuity that makes the poetry of Herrick so enduring. The relationship with Nature is one of those everlasting relationships that humanity is perpetually dealing with (like the relation to the body, to God, to politics). In his poetry Herrick tackles the great themes – love, time, God, Nature, the body.

Much of Herrick's poetry concerns the themes and imagery of Elizabethan (and mediæval) poetry: the evocation of a pastoral, Arcadian, pre-sinful landscape, a Paradise, in fact, populated with shepherdesses, nymphs, animals and the abundance of Nature. Already in Shakespeare this pastoral mythology was fading, being supplanted by a worldly knowingness (if not cynicism). Herrick's poetry, though, often harks back to a paradisal earlier age, and rues the passing of time that has changed it all (for the worse, in his opinion). We find the same Greek, Roman, Biblical, mediæval, Christian and Renaissance/ humanist themes in Herrick's work that are the staple of Elizabethan poetry.[5] As well as learned and literary, Herrick's subjects are often seemingly 'ordinary' or 'common-place'. He writes of bucolic traditions; of old age; of bawdy times; of his mistress's breasts; of cherry blossom; of fashionable clothes (one of his famous poems is 'Delight in Disorder', where 'a careless shoestring' betokens a 'wild civility' which 'bewitches' the poet more than precision).

There are many poems in Herrick's work of love – about love desired, lost and mourned. Herrick is very definitely a 'Muse poet', to use Robert Graves's term. There are many poems to various mistresses, 'my dearest Beauties' he calls them in 'To His Lovely Mistresses' (Anthea, Perilla, Electra, Blanch, Judith, Silvia, and the most beloved of all, Julia). There are many poems to certain 'muses' or 'maidens'. The sheer number (and quality) of Herrick's poems to Julia attests to his deep passion for women, the friendship and strength of women: 'To Julia', 'To Roses in Julia's Bosom', 'To the Fever Not to Trouble Julia', 'Julia's Petticoat', 'The Frozen Zone: or, Julia Disdainful', 'To Julia, in Her Dawn, or Daybreak', 'His Last Request to Julia', 'The Parliament of Roses to Julia', 'Upon Julia's Recovery', 'Upon Julia's Fall', 'His Sailing From Julia', 'His Embalming to Julia', 'Her Legs', 'Her Bed', 'On Julia's Picture', 'The Bracelet to Julia', 'A Ring Presented to Julia', 'To Julia in the Temple' and so on. Apart from poems addressed 'To His Book', there are probably more poems in Herrick's work 'To Julia' than to anything else. Julia is 'the prime of *Paradise'* ('To Julia, in Her Dawn, or Day- breake'). She is utterly adored, often erotically. There are many poems which eulogize her breasts and nipples, for instance: 'Display thy breasts.../ Between whose glories, there my lips I'll lay,/ Ravisht' he writes (in 'Upon Julia's Breasts'); other pæans to Julia's breasts include 'Upon the Roses in Julia's Bosom' and 'Upon the Nipples of Julia's Breast'. Herrick makes the age-old connections between the fertility of Nature outside (the rain, the lush vegetation, the rivers of the Paradisal Earth) and the bounty of women inside (Julia's breasts form a valley of abundance, as in Shakespeare's 'Venus and Adonis', in which the poet would like to languish). Women in Herrick's poetry are seen as the givers of pleasure (expressed as sex), nurturance (breast milk), and all things worthy in the world (love). 'All Pleasures meet in Woman- kind' he writes in 'On Himself'. They are just as important in his poetry as God, the King or Christianity. Much of Herrick's poetry concerns (masculine) public, worldly, and religious themes (such as King Charles and politics, or God and the Bible), but just as much (more, probably) celebrates (feminine) erotic pleasure, food, Nature, folk rituals, music and women, in that 'cleanly-wanton' way which is Herrick's own (the phrase, which describes much of his work, comes from the opening poem of

Hesperides).

Herrick happily fuses erotic descriptions of Nature or food with lush, sensual evocations of erotic love.6 To describe how wonderful sensual love can be, Herrick, like so many poets before him, uses the metaphor of abundant Nature, expressed in flowers, trees, rivers, hills, and food. In 'To Phillis To love, and Love With Him', for example, Herrick's narrator proclaims:

Live, live with me, and thou shalt see
The pleasures I'll prepare for thee...

And goes into a long list of the bounty of Nature: 'sweet soft Moss shall by thy bed', 'Fleeces purest Downe', 'Cream of Cowslips buttered', daisies, violets, daffodils, primroses, roses, the 'blushing Apple, bashful Peare,/ And shame-fac't Plum'. Herrick's poetry is, like Shelley's or Shakespeare's, tremendously sensual. In poem after poem he uses metaphors and images of shiny, ripe fruit, or radiant flowers, or soft grass, or silk, or fresh springwater. Images of natural abundance occur throughout his poetry. Even rain, which he would have known day after day in Dartmoor, is treated spectrally, as in 'A Conjuration to Electra', where he speaks of the 'Dewes and drisling Raine,/ That swell the Golden Graine'. Some of the most erotic poems around concerning perfume and smell are Herrick's: In 'Love Perfumes All Parts' Herrick writes of his mistress Anthea's body in a state of heightened intoxication, claiming that her hands, thighs and legs 'are all/ Richly Aromatical'. So deliciously musky is the beloved for the poet, he says she is sweeter than Juno and muskier than the Goddess Isis, no less.

Some of Herrick's best landscape poems are not about Dartmoor or Devonshire, but about London, his birthplace and beloved city. 'His Return to London' is perhaps the best of these city-poems, in which his return to the capital is seen as a yearned-for homecoming.

> O *Place! O People!* Manners! fram'd to please
> All *Nations, Customers, Kindreds, Language!*

There are poems in Herrick's *œuvre* on the pleasures of music, which he calls 'thou *Queen of Heaven,* Care-charming-spel' (in 'To Musick. A Song'). The theme of the music-poems is the enchantment that music can bring. 'Charm me asleep, and melt me so/ With thy Delicious Numbers' he urges music in 'To Musique, To Becalme His Fever'. 'And make me smooth as Balme, and Oile againe' he entreats in 'To Musick'.

There are some hearty and tender pæans to holidays, feasts, festivals and rituals (pagan as well as Christian) in Herrick's poetry: such as 'The Succession of Four Sweet Months', and the best of them all, Corinna's Going a Maying'. The celebration of the seasons and annual holidays chimes with Herrick's abiding theme of the passing of time, and the need to seize the moment and enjoy it.

Some of Herrick's most delightful poems are about the wonders of Nature, such as blossoms, flowers and fields ('The Shower of Blossoms', 'The Lilly in a Christal', 'To Pansies', 'To Cherry-blossomes', 'To a Bed of Tulips', 'To Laurels', 'Upon Roses, 'The Succession of Four Sweet Months', 'The Rainbow', 'To the Rose: Song', 'To Flowers', 'To Blossoms', 'To Groves', 'To Violets', 'To Carnations', 'To Sycamores', 'To Springs and Fountains', 'To Daffadills', 'To Meddowes', 'To the Willow-tree' and 'To Prim-roses Fill'd With Morning-dew').

It's typical of Herrick, too, to mention in his Nature poems the passing of time. The very first verse of his 'To Blossoms' asks the question of the blossoms 'Why do ye fall so fast?' As soon as the beauty of the blossoms is invoked, time and death follow on immediately. The line of 'To Blossoms' is 'They glide/ Into the grave.' The same protestations to Nature's pleasures being over so swiftly occur in 'To Daisies, Not To Shut So Soone' and 'To Daffadills' ('we weep to see/ You haste away so soone'). In 'All Things Decay and Die' he states quite baldly: *'All things decay with Time'*.

The many poems 'To His Book' attest to Herrick's deep concern for his art – how long (or if) it will last, who will enshrine it, and soon. The same concerns with the relations between mortality, time and death and the artist and his art are central to Shakespeare's *œuvre* (it is the guiding theme of the *Sonnets*). The key Herrick theme is to enjoy life before death takes it away. 'While Fate permits us, let's be merry' as he puts it in 'To Enjoy the Time'. 'Every time seems so short to be' he says in 'Felicity, Quick of Flight'.

It's true that Robert Herrick did not write long poems, like Shelley or Wordsworth (in the sense that long, 'epic' poems equal seriousness and *gravitas*),[7] but, in his own way, his Nature poetry is every bit as valuable as theirs. His love-poetry is sometimes compared unfavourably with that of John Donne: again, in his own way, Herrick is every bit as fruitful a love-poet as Donne (or Campion, Marlowe, even Shakespeare or Spenser). He was not as showy a poet as Coleridge or Pope, not so ambitious, formally, yet he is a superb writer, witty, hedonistic, impassioned, commonsensical.

I have modernized some of the spellings in Herrick's poems, but have kept his capitalizations and use of italics. These are part of the flavour of Herrick's verse, and do not detract, I think, from the power or nuance of his poetry. I have chosen more of his poems from the secular book *Hesperides* than from the religious volume *Noble Numbers*, not only because there are simply many more poems in *Hesperides*, but also because *Hesperides* contains his best work.

Notes

1. F.R. Leavis: *Revaluation*, Chatto & Windus 1936, 36
2. T.S. Eliot: "What is Minor Poetry?", *Swanee Review*, 54, 1946
3. Leah S. Marcus: "Robert Herrick", in Coms, 1993, 180
4. In 'Discontents in Devon' Herrick writes:

More discontents I never had
Since I was born, then here;
Where I have been, and still am sad,
In this dull *Devon-shire*...

5. In his poetry Herrick alludes to, among others, Anacreon, Horace, Catullus, Marital and other (Roman) poets, as well as Ben Jonson (whom Herrick admired) and the *Bible*.

6. As Stephen Coote puts it, in Herrick's poetry the 'sensuousness is the more telling for its sophisticated simplicity and, at its best, is returned to nature.' (Coote: *The Penguin Short History of English Literature*, Penguin 1993, 175)

7. There are lengthy poems (such as 'Upon His Kinswoman Mistress Elizabeth Herrick', 'His Age, Dedicated To His Peculiar Friend, M. John Wickes, Under the Name of Posthumus', 'A Nuptial Song, or Epithalamie, on Sir Clipseby Crew and His Lady', 'Corinna's Going a Maying', 'A Country Life: To His Brother, M. Tho: Herrick', 'The Welcome to Sack' and 'An Epithalamie to Sir Thomas Southwell and His Ladie') but nothing as long as *Prometheus Unbound* or *The Replude*.

Bibliography

Cleanth Brooks: *The Well Wrought Urn*, Dennis Dobson 1957

A.B. Coiro: *Robert Herrick's 'Hesperides' and the Epigram Book Tradition*, John Hopkins University Press 1988

—ed: *Robert Herrick*, special no. of *George Herbert Journal* 14, 1-2, Autumn 1990

N. Coms, ed: *The Cambridge Companion to English Poetry: Donne to Marvell*, Cambridge University Press 1993

R.H. Deming: *Ceremony and Art: Robert Herrick's Poetry*, Mouton, Hague 1974

A. Leigh Deneef: *'This Poetick Liturgie': Robert Herrick's Ceremonial Mode*, Duke University Press 1974

E.H. Hageman: *Robert Herrick: A Reference Guide*, G.K. Hall, Boston 1983

G. Hammond: *Fleeting Things: English Poets and Poems 1616-1660*, Harvard University Press 1990

Robert Herrick: *The Poems of Robert Herrick*, ed. L.C. Martin, Oxford University Press 1965

—*Poems*, ed. J. Max Patrick, New York University Press 1963

—*Robert Herrick: The Hesperides and Noble Numbers*, ed. Alfred Pollard, Muse's Library, London 1891

—*The Poetical Works of Robert Herrick,* Oxford English Texts 1915

—*Hesperides: The Poems and Other Remains of Robert Herrick Now First Collected*, ed. W. Carew Hazlitt, London 1869

—*The Complete Works of Robert Herrick*, ed. Alexander B. Grosart, London 1876

—*Selected Poems*, ed. David Jesson-Dibley, Carcanet 1989

M. MacLeod: *Concordance to the Poems of Robert Herrick*, Oxford University Press, New York 1936

Leah S. Marcus: *The Politics of Mirth: Jonson, Herrick, Milton, Marvell and the Defense of Old Holiday Pastimes*, University of Chicago Press 1986

F.W. Moorman: *Robert Herrick: a Biographical and Critical Study*, Russell & Russell, New York 1910

S. Musgrove: "The Universe of Robert Herrick", *Auckland University College Bulletin*, 38, 1950

John Press: *Herrick*, Longmans, Green & Co
Roger Rollin: *Robert Herrick*, Twayne, New York 1966/92
—& J. Max Patrick, eds: *Trust to Good Verses: Herrick Tercentenary Essays*, University of Pittsburgh Press 1977
George W. Scott: *Robert Herrick,* Sidgwick & Jackson 1974

J.R.R. Tolkien
The Books, The Films, The Whole Cultural Phenomenon

by Jeremy Mark Robinson

A new critical study of J.R.R. Tolkien, creator of Middle-earth and author of *The Lord of the Rings, The Hobbit* and *The Silmarillion*, among other books.

This new critical study explores Tolkien's major writings (*The Lord of the Rings, The Hobbit, Beowulf: The Monster and the Critics, The Letters, The Silmarillion* and *The History of Middle-earth* volumes); Tolkien and fairy tales; the mythological, political and religious aspects of Tolkien's Middle-earth; the critics' response to Tolkien's fiction over the decades; the Tolkien industry (merchandizing, toys, role-playing games, posters, Tolkien societies, conferences and the like); Tolkien in visual and fantasy art; the cultural aspects of The Lord of the Rings (from the 1950s to the present); Tolkien's fiction's relationship with other fantasy fiction, such as C.S. Lewis and *Harry Potter*; and the TV, radio and film versions of Tolkien's books, including the 2001-03 Hollywood interpretations of *The Lord of the Rings*.

This new book draws on contemporary cultural theory and analysis and offers a sympathetic and illuminating (and sceptical) account of the Tolkien phenomenon. This book is designed to appeal to the general reader (and viewer) of Tolkien: it is written in a clear, jargon-free and easily-accessible style.

754pp   ISBN 1-86171-057-7   £25.00 / $37.50

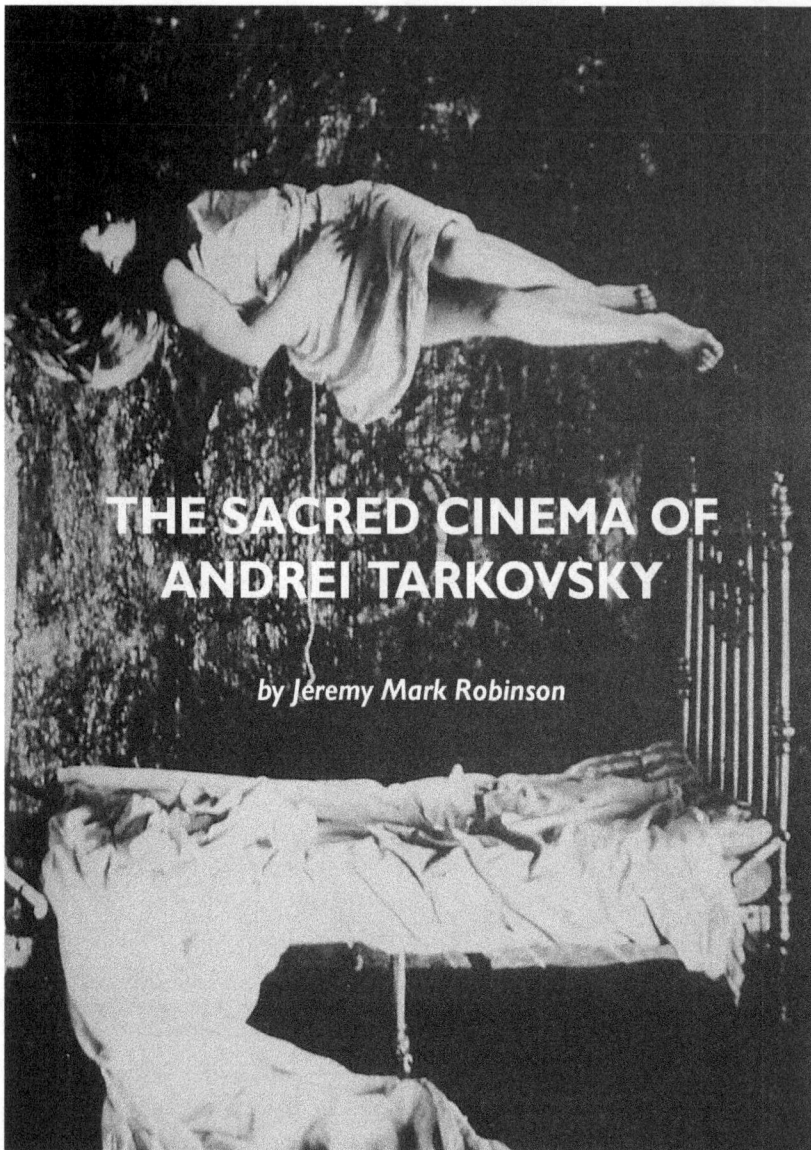

THE SACRED CINEMA OF
ANDREI TARKOVSKY

by Jeremy Mark Robinson

A new study of the Russian filmmaker Andrei Tarkovsky (1932-1986), director of seven feature films, including *Andrei Roublyov, Mirror, Solaris, Stalker* and *The Sacrifice*.

This is one of the most comprehensive and detailed studies of Tarkovsky's cinema available. Every film is explored in depth, with scene-by-scene analyses. All aspects of Tarkovsky's output are critiqued, including editing, camera, staging, script, budget, collaborations, production, sound, music, performance and spirituality. Tarkovsky is placed with a European New Wave tradition of filmmaking, alongside directors like Ingmar Bergman, Carl Theodor Dreyer, Pier Paolo Pasolini and Robert Bresson.

An essential addition to film studies.

Illustrations: 150 b/w, 4 colour. 682 pages. First edition. Hardback.

Publisher: Crescent Moon Publishing. Distributor: Gardners Books.

ISBN 1-86171-096-8 (9781861710963) £60.00 / $105.00

THE ART OF
ANDY GOLDSWORTHY

COMPLETE WORKS: SPECIAL EDITION
(PAPERBACK and HARDBACK)

by William Malpas

A new, special edition of the study of the contemporary British sculptor,
Andy Goldsworthy, including a new introduction, new bibliography and many
new illustrations.

This is the most comprehensive, up-to-date, well-researched and in-depth
account of Goldsworthy's art available anywhere.

Andy Goldsworthy makes land art. His sculpture is a sensitive, intuitive
response to nature, light, time, growth, the seasons and the earth. Goldswor-
thy's environmental art is becoming ever more popular: 1993's art book
Stone was a bestseller; the press raved about Goldsworthy taking over a
number of London West End art galleries in 1994; during 1995 Goldsworthy
designed a set of Royal Mail stamps and had a show at the British Museum.
Malpas surveys all of Goldsworthy's art, and analyzes his relation with other
land artists such as Robert Smithson, Walter de Maria, Richard Long and
David Nash, and his place in the contemporary British art scene.

The Art of Andy Goldsworthy discusses all of Goldsworthy's important and
recent exhibitions and books, including the *Sheepfolds* project; the TV docu-
mentaries; *Wood* (1996); the New York Holocaust memorial (2003); and
Goldsworthy's collaboration on a dance performance.

Illustrations: 70 b/w, 1 colour. 330 pages. New, special, 2nd edition.
Publisher: Crescent Moon Publishing. Distributor: Gardners Books.

ISBN 1-86171-059-3 (9781861710598) (Paperback) £25.00 / $44.00

ISBN 1-86171-080-1 (9781861710802) (Hardback) £60.00 / $105.00

CRESCENT MOON PUBLISHING

ARTS, PAINTING, SCULPTURE

The Art of Andy Goldsworthy: Complete Works(Pbk)
The Art of Andy Goldsworthy: Complete Works (Hbk)
Andy Goldsworthy in Close-Up (Pbk)
Andy Goldsworthy in Close-Up (Hbk)
Land Art: A Complete Guide
Richard Long: The Art of Walking
The Art of Richard Long: Complete Works (Pbk)
The Art of Richard Long: Complete Works (Hbk)
Richard Long in Close-Up
Land Art In the UK
Land Art in Close-Up
Installation Art in Close-Up
Minimal Art and Artists In the 1960s and After
Colourfield Painting
Land Art DVD, TV documentary
Andy Goldsworthy DVD, TV documentary
The Erotic Object: Sexuality in Sculpture From Prehistory to the Present Day
Sex in Art: Pornography and Pleasure in Painting and Sculpture
Postwar Art
Sacred Gardens: The Garden in Myth, Religion and Art
Glorification: Religious Abstraction in Renaissance and 20th Century Art
Early Netherlandish Painting
Leonardo da Vinci
Piero della Francesca
Giovanni Bellini
Fra Angelico: Art and Religion in the Renaissance
Mark Rothko: The Art of Transcendence
Frank Stella: American Abstract Artist
Jasper Johns: Painting By Numbers
Brice Marden
Alison Wilding: The Embrace of Sculpture
Vincent van Gogh: Visionary Landscapes
Eric Gill: Nuptials of God
Constantin Brancusi: Sculpting the Essence of Things
Max Beckmann
Egon Schiele: Sex and Death In Purple Stockings
Delizioso Fotografico Fervore: Works In Process 1
Sacro Cuore: Works In Process 2
The Light Eternal: J.M.W. Turner
The Madonna Glorified: Karen Arthurs

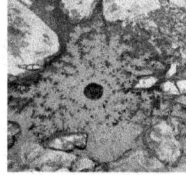

LITERATURE

J.R.R. Tolkien: The Books, The Films, The Whole Cultural Phenomenon
Harry Potter
Sexing Hardy: Thomas Hardy and Feminism
Thomas Hardy's *Tess of the d'Urbervilles*
Thomas Hardy's *Jude the Obscure*
Thomas Hardy: The Tragic Novels
Love and Tragedy: Thomas Hardy
The Poetry of Landscape in Hardy
Wessex Revisited: Thomas Hardy and John Cowper Powys
Wolfgang Iser: Essays
Petrarch, Dante and the Troubadours
Maurice Sendak and the Art of Children's Book Illustration
Andrea Dworkin
Cixous, Irigaray, Kristeva: The *Jouissance* of French Feminism
Julia Kristeva: Art, Love, Melancholy, Philosophy, Semiotics and Psychoanalysis
Hélene Cixous I Love You: The *Jouissance* of Writing
Luce Irigaray: Lips, Kissing, and the Politics of Sexual Difference
Peter Redgrove: Here Comes the Flood
Peter Redgrove: Sex-Magic-Poetry-Cornwall
Lawrence Durrell: Between Love and Death, East and West
Love, Culture & Poetry: Lawrence Durrell
Cavafy: Anatomy of a Soul
German Romantic Poetry: Goethe, Novalis, Heine, Hölderlin, Schlegel, Schiller
Feminism and Shakespeare
Shakespeare: Selected Sonnets
Shakespeare: Love, Poetry & Magic
The Passion of D.H. Lawrence
D.H. Lawrence: Symbolic Landscapes
D.H. Lawrence: Infinite Sensual Violence
Rimbaud: Arthur Rimbaud and the Magic of Poetry
The Ecstasies of John Cowper Powys
Sensualism and Mythology: The Wessex Novels of John Cowper Powys
Amorous Life: John Cowper Powys and the Manifestation of Affectivity (H.W. Fawkner)
Postmodern Powys: New Essays on John Cowper Powys (Joe Boulter)
Rethinking Powys: Critical Essays on John Cowper Powys
Paul Bowles & Bernardo Bertolucci
Rainer Maria Rilke
In the Dim Void: Samuel Beckett
Samuel Beckett Goes into the Silence
André Gide: Fiction and Fervour
Jackie Collins and the Blockbuster Novel
Blinded By Her Light: The Love-Poetry of Robert Graves
The Passion of Colours: Travels In Mediterranean Lands
Poetic Forms
The Dolphin-Boy

POETRY

The Best of Peter Redgrove's Poetry
Peter Redgrove: Here Comes The Flood
Peter Redgrove: Sex-Magic-Poetry-Cornwall
Ursula Le Guin: Walking In Cornwall
Dante: Selections From the Vita Nuova
Petrarch, Dante and the Troubadours
William Shakespeare: Selected Sonnets
Blinded By Her Light: The Love-Poetry of Robert Graves
Emily Dickinson: Selected Poems
Emily Brontë: Poems
Thomas Hardy: Selected Poems
Percy Bysshe Shelley: Poems
John Keats: Selected Poems
D.H. Lawrence: Selected Poems
Edmund Spenser: Poems
John Donne: Poems
Henry Vaughan: Poems
Sir Thomas Wyatt: Poems
Robert Herrick: Selected Poems
Rilke: Space, Essence and Angels in the Poetry of Rainer Maria Rilke
Rainer Maria Rilke: Selected Poems
Friedrich Hölderlin: Selected Poems
Arseny Tarkovsky: Selected Poems
Arthur Rimbaud: Selected Poems
Arthur Rimbaud: A Season in Hell
Arthur Rimbaud and the Magic of Poetry
D.J. Enright: By-Blows
Jeremy Reed: Brigitte's Blue Heart
Jeremy Reed: Claudia Schiffer's Red Shoes
Gorgeous Little Orpheus
Radiance: New Poems
Crescent Moon Book of Nature Poetry
Crescent Moon Book of Love Poetry
Crescent Moon Book of Mystical Poetry
Crescent Moon Book of Elizabethan Love Poetry
Crescent Moon Book of Metaphysical Poetry
Crescent Moon Book of Romantic Poetry
Pagan America: New American Poetry

MEDIA, CINEMA, FEMINISM and CULTURAL STUDIES

J.R.R. Tolkien: The Books, The Films, The Whole Cultural Phenomenon
Harry Potter
Cixous, Irigaray, Kristeva: The *Jouissance* of French Feminism
Julia Kristeva: Art, Love, Melancholy, Philosophy, Semiotics and Psychoanalysis
Luce Irigaray: Lips, Kissing, and the Politics of Sexual Difference
Hélene Cixous I Love You: The *Jouissance* of Writing
Andrea Dworkin
'Cosmo Woman': The World of Women's Magazines
Women in Pop Music
Discovering the Goddess (Geoffrey Ashe)
The Poetry of Cinema
The Sacred Cinema of Andrei Tarkovsky (Pbk and Hbk)
Paul Bowles & Bernardo Bertolucci
Media Hell: Radio, TV and the Press
An Open Letter to the BBC
Detonation Britain: Nuclear War in the UK
Feminism and Shakespeare
Wild Zones: Pornography, Art and Feminism
Sex in Art: Pornography and Pleasure in Painting and Sculpture
Sexing Hardy: Thomas Hardy and Feminism

In my view *The Light Eternal* is among the very best of all the material I read on Turner. (Douglas Graham, director of the Turner Museum, Denver, Colorado)

The Light Eternal is a model monograph, an exemplary job. The subject matter of the book is beautifully organised and dead on beam. (Lawrence Durrell)

It is amazing for me to see my work treated with such passion and respect. (Andrea Dworkin)

Sex-Magic-Poetry-Cornwall is a very rich essay... It is like a brightly-lighted box. (Peter Redgrove)

CRESCENT MOON PUBLISHING
P.O. Box 393, Maidstone, Kent, ME14 5XU, United Kingdom.
01622-729593 (UK) 01144-1622-729593 (US) 0044-1622-729593 (other territories)
cresmopub@yahoo.co.uk   www.crescentmoon.org.uk

www.ingramcontent.com/pod-product-compliance
Lightning Source LLC
Chambersburg PA
CBHW062006040426
42447CB00010B/1937